HANDI GRACE

TALKING TOGETHER ABOUT GOD

HANDLING GRACE

TALKING TOGETHER ABOUT GOD

DR KEN BAKER

ELIM MINISTRIES, IRELAND

Printed in Ireland

First Printing, 2016

ISBN 978-1-326-50238-6

Elim Ministries Publishing
22 The Haven, Roscrea

Co.Tipperary

IRELAND

www.tithebarn.wordpress.com

Foreword

"Oh, the depth of the riches
of the wisdom and knowledge of God!

How unsearchable his judgments,
and his paths beyond tracing out!
'Who has known the mind of the Lord?
Or who has been his counsellor?
'Who has ever given to God,
that God should repay them?

For from him and through him
and for him are all things.
To him be the glory for ever! Amen."
(Romans 11:33-36)

The word "theology" comes from two Greek words that combined mean "talking together about God." In the letter to the Romans, Paul offers a sustained theology of the Gospel of Christ. But he pauses mid-lecture (as it were) and breaks off into this song of praise. It's a powerful and profound moment that indicates four important principles about the study of theology. The first is that **it is shaped by praise.** Theology is always devotional. It can never be dry, academic or nit-picking. We are not theatre-critics, pens poised for acerbic comment; we are the children in the balcony, mouths open in wonder. "*To him be the glory for ever! Amen.*"

The second principle in this passage that governs the study of theology is that **it is anchored in Christ**. Paul had no New Testament, of course, but with skill and precision he wove passages from the Hebrew Bible, from the long history of Israel together into a coherent Christ-centred whole. Jesus is the hub, the centre of the wheel, and every spoke connects to him. *"For from him and through him and for him are all things."*

The third principle about the study of theology, you may be surprised to hear, is that **it is incomplete.** *"How unsearchable his judgments, and his paths beyond tracing out!"* Christian theology is simply an attempt to understand God as he is revealed in the Bible, but *'Who has known the mind oj the Lord? Or who has been his counsellor? 'Who has ever given to God, that God should repay them?"* We are out of our depth, immediately, squinting through a fog at blurred outlines. We see "*through a glass darkly*" but yet we are called to love God with our minds.

This principle saves us from arrogance, from that fatal sense of thinking that it is our job to nail everything down, and then stand arms akimbo, satisfied that the job is now done. It was the mistake that the Pharisees made.

John Wesley said "Bring me a worm that can comprehend man and I'll show you a man who can comprehend God."

The fourth principle implied in this passage is that **the study of theology is relational.** It is a highly significant "We" who are "talking together about God," in a conversation shaped by praise, and anchored in Christ.

So theology has a corporate significance. The mutual, devotional, Christ-centred study of God is, precisely, how we love God with our minds. It's part of our worship, our "reasonable service," our obedience, and our evangelism to work together to explain the ways of God to our generation.

And God himself is relational. When Moses asked who was sending him to Pharaoh, God replied "I AM WHO I AM" (Exodus 3:14). The name I AM indicates personality. God has a name, even as he has given names to others. The name I AM stands for a free, purposeful, self-sufficient personality. God is not an ethereal force or a cosmic energy. He is the almighty, self-existing, self-determining Being with a mind and a will—through his Word, and through his Son, Jesus Christ.

And "*To him be the glory for ever! Amen.*"

***

This booklet was prepared as a series of discussion starters for use with the Theology Lectures of the Elim Academy, Dublin, 2016.

Rev Dr Ken Baker

1. Who is God?

"In the beginning God created the heavens and the earth."(Genesis 1:1)

The Bible begins with an emphatic answer to the title question "Who is God?" God just **is,** before anything else. But even that word "is" implies personality. That is to say, there is an immediate insistence on the personality of God. So "Who is God?" is a good question. If we were to ask, "*What* is God?" we might be tempted to say that God is the infinite being, the creator, a presence, or something like that. These answers may be partially correct, but the title question brings us closer to what the Bible teaches.

Is God a he?

There is no question of gender in God, of course, even though the limitations of the English language force us to use the words "he" "his" now and then. If gender does come into the mind of the Hebrew writers then it is strongly paternal rather than patriarchal (the loving, protective father rather than the stern tribal chief).

But the key to the gender issue is in Genesis 1:27: *"God created mankind in his own image, in the image of God he created them; male and female he created them."* This is a crucial verse which repays a lot of thought, but for now it's enough to notice that the "*image of God*" is "*both male and female.*" The differentiation of gender, (*male and female*), are **both** perfectly expressed in what the writer means by "God."

In the same context comes another enriching principle. The word used for "God" through Genesis 1 is a plural term. Usually, this plural usage is said to express strength and authority in Hebrew, but in v26, the creative activity of God is also described as plurality: *"Then God said, 'Let us make mankind in our image, in our likeness.' "* God is described as an "us."

This usage recalls the first verses of the Bible: *"In the beginning God created...the Spirit of God was hovering over the waters. And God said.."*

Isn't it interesting to consider the three-fold activity of God in creation? God makes, God hovers, God speaks. He is maker, midwife, and communicator. The insistence on the oneness of God was something the Jews defended to the death, (literally). Isaiah pronounced it like a clarion-call: "*I am the Lord, and there is no other; Besides me there is no God,"* (Isaiah 45:5). And yet, here in the very opening sequence of the Hebrew text, there is this suggestion of community-in-action which is the very heart of what has come to be called the doctrine of" trinity."

The word "trinity" simply means "threeness." This means that God exists in three persons, not three gods. Technically, the doctrine of the Trinity states that in the one God is the person of the Father, the Son, and the Holy Spirit. Each is not the same person as the other, yet there are not three gods but one. Think of time. Time is past, present, and future. The past is not the same as the present, which is not the same as the future. But, there are not three times. There is only one thing called time.

The reason the word, "person," is used in describing the Father, the Son, and the Holy Spirit is because each exhibits attributes of personhood, not in terms of physicality but of personality. In other words, each has a will, and each loves, speaks, is aware of others, communicates with others, etc. These are attributes of personhood, and we see the Father, the Son, and the Holy Spirit each demonstrating these qualities.

The Bible does not use the term "trinity" but does suggest it here and there. For example:

In Matthew 28:19: "*Go therefore and make disciples of all the nations, baptizing them in the name of the Father and the Son and the Holy Spirit.*"

In 2 Corinthians 13:14, *"The grace of the Lord Jesus Christ, and the love of God, and the fellowship of the Holy Spirit, be with you all."*

The implication is that these Three have their very being in their inter-relationship. It's an analogy of loving, purposive community. In Mark Driscoll and Gerry Breshears book, *Doctrine: What Christians Should Believe,* seven practical implications are drawn from the doctrine of the trinity, developing this idea of trinity-as-community.

Trinitarian life is humble. The doctrine of the Trinity is so complex and wonderfully mysterious that it humbles us. This is because while God can be known truly, he cannot be known fully. This forces us to be humble in our understanding of God and establishes a precedent in our thinking to allow room for mystery, as we indeed see and know in part, as Scripture states.

Trinitarian life is loving. When 1 John 4:7 says, *"Love is from God,"* it is revealing that love emanates from the Trinitarian community of God. Trinitarian love includes love for God, family, friend, neighbour, stranger, and even enemy. This is because even though we were enemies of God, estranged by sin, Jesus came to be our neighbour, loved us as a friend, died for our sins to make us family, and shared with us God's love.

Trinitarian life is worshipful. This means that we worship, including singing, serving, and praying, to the Father, through the Son, by the power of the Holy Spirit.

Trinitarian life is relational. John 1:1 says, "*In the beginning was the Word* (Jesus), *and the Word was with God* (Father), *and the Word was God.*" In the original Greek, John is saying that God the Father and God the Son were proverbially face-to-face in eternity past. This is the language of friendship, which compels us to live face-to-face with others in companionship and community. This is why Christians practice hospitality to strangers and whey they participate in the life of their local church as they live face-to-face with their spouses and children. All of this is to practice for the day when, as Paul says, we too will see God "face-to-face."

Trinitarian life is unified and diverse. Greek Christian theologians are fond of describing the Trinity with the term *perichoresis.* As the three persons of the Trinity are mutually indwelling, or permeating one another, we are deeply connected as part of the body, yet we retain our own identity. We are always persons in community.

Trinitarian life is submissive. As we hear Jesus teaching us to pray, "*Your will be done,*" and himself praying, "*Not my will, but yours, be done,*" we learn to submit ourselves to the will of the Father, by the Spirit like the Son.

Trinitarian life is joyful. The Trinity is the place of the greatest joy that has ever been or ever will be; each member of the Trinity (Father, Son, Spirit), delights in the others and pours himself out continuously for the good of the others. Some religions teach that God made people to cure his loneliness; conversely, the fact is that God as a

Trinitarian community was never without joyful and loving community. He is a relational God who welcomes us into a joyful and loving relationship with himself.

The Trinity is not a doctrine to be philosophized beyond the teachings of Scripture but rather a humble, loving, worshipful, relational, diverse, submissive, and joyful life to entered into by the Spirit through the Son to the Father.

REFLECTIVE QUESTIONS

- What do you understand by the following phrases:

  "Theology is always devotional."

  "Christian Theology is anchored in Christ."

  "Theology is relational."

- Why is theology "necessarily incomplete"?

- What do you think are the implications of the doctrine of the Trinity for the way we live as Christians today?

2. How does God reveal himself? –By his words

"And the Word became flesh and dwelt amongst us." (John 1:14)

God is a communicator. The most characteristic phrase of Genesis 1 is "*And God said.*" There are three attributes of this communicability that I'd like to emphasise here.

It is personal. It is authentic. It is a secure foundation for life.

First, **it is personal.**

John Henry Newman wrote "I sought to hear the voice of God and climbed the topmost steeple, but God declared: "Go down again – I dwell among the people."

The God of the Bible is not afar off, nor is he difficult to reach. The whole wonder of the incarnation is that God came to us. But to the readers of the first century, this verse from the opening chapter of John's gospel was packed with much more meaning.

It meant that the thinking processes of God were being made comprehensible; that the wisdom of God was being unpacked; that the communication of God was now coming through loud and clear. It was as if a long-distorted radio signal was now tweaked into clarity.

The word is coming through!

So that means that God's voice could be understood and acted upon. If "*the word became flesh*" then God had become interactive, participatory, conversational! God was providing an audio-message to show the way through the puzzle of life.

And Jesus said "*I am the way, the truth and the life.*" God provides the direction I need to go, the instructions I need to know, and the only satisfying kind of existence I need to experience.

And this is how we approach the Bible, as the speaking voice of God, as the word of God, authoritative and relevant.

So, second, **it is authentic.**

It is the claim of 2 Timothy 3:16 that "*All scripture is inspired by God.*" 2 Peter 1:21 adds that "*No prophecy was ever made by an act of human will but men moved by the Holy Spirit spoke from God.*" Jesus uses the words of the Old Testament in the same terms, as if God is speaking (and we better listen!).

This authenticity is confirmed by the Holy Spirit. John 16:13 states, "*But when He, the Spirit of truth comes, He will guide you into all truth.*" The Holy Spirit, that is to say, takes what is given and leads us further, like a good Guide, into authentic living.

This authenticity is further demonstrated by the Bible's power to transform lives. Hebrews 4:12 says, "*The word of God is living and active and sharper than any two-edged sword, and piercing as far as the division of soul and spirit.*"

Romans 12:2 says, "*And be not conformed to this world but be transformed by the renewing of your mind.*"

The Word of God and the Spirit of God actually transforms the lives of people. No other book can make such a claim. This is because the Bible is not a mere book on good living but is literally packed with power. It is the Word of God with the power to change lives.

Third, **it is a secure foundation for life.** There is a solidity about the Word of God that is very reassuring.

"Heaven and earth will pass away, but my words will not pass away." Luke 21:33.

It's like crossing a stream, stretching cautiously to see whether a rock will support you, and then discovering that it will!

When we come to ask our Father something upon the authority of his word, then we have found that solid rock beneath our feet. So our prayers should be guided by the Word of God. As we study the Bible to gain understanding and to learn about God's nature, we will have more confidence and direction in prayer.

Nehemiah –for example- based his prayer on what he knew of God's nature and on the promises in God's Word:

"'Lord, the God of heaven, the great and awesome God, who keeps his covenant of love with those who love him and keep his commandments, let your ear be attentive and your eyes open to hear the prayer your servant is praying..." (Nehemiah 1:5,6)

Gandhi once wrote: "Prayer is not asking. It is a longing of the soul. It is daily admission of one's weakness. It is better in prayer to have a heart without words than words without a heart." But my "weakness" requires the solidity of his words to find a safe place to stand. And that place is eternally secure. His *"words will not pass away"*!

Lord, I receive it.

REFLECTIVE QUESTIONS

- How important is it to receive the Bible as the authoritative word of a living God?
- What do you think about this sentence: "My "weakness" requires the solidity of his words to find a safe place to stand."
- How has the Bible changed your life?

3. How does God reveal himself?–By his works

"By the word of the Lord the heavens were made; And by the breath of His mouth all their hosts. ... For He spoke, and it was done; He commanded and it stood fast." (Psalm 33:6,9)

The Bible is clear: God made all things out of nothing with a sovereign word of command. The film director shouts "Lights! Action!" and his word calls it into being.

There some important consequences to this concept. First, it keeps a distance between Creator and Creation. It's as small as the distance between speaker and the word spoken, but that's the point: it ascribes contingency (or dependency) to what is said (and done) and authority, power and ownership to the One-Who-Speaks.

There are two wonderful words that have been used to explore this difference between the Speaker and the Word Spoken. Though God is separate from His creation and stands above it in his *transcendence*, at the same time He is intimately involved in the world He has made in His *immanence*.

A distinguishing characteristic of the Biblical view of life is that God is a God who comes, a God who visits his people, a God who breaks into history and human lives and performs mighty deeds: *"Praise him for his acts of power; praise him for his surpassing greatness."* Ps 150: 2).

But let's consider not that "breaking and entering" into history (of which, more later!) but this statement:

Creation shows who God is and what he is like.

He is not an absentee Creator who merely "watches us from a distance" or a clockmaker, who, having finished his word, stands back to see it working. Rather, God is fully engaged with what he has made and reveals himself through it and in it.

As Psalm 104:24 puts it: "*O Lord, how many are Your works! In wisdom You have made them all; the earth is full of Your possessions*". God's sheer brilliance is on display in everything He has made! We appreciate his wisdom in the tiniest aspect of what he has made. I met a haematologist who came to Christ through a study of blood samples. The sheer purposiveness of such intricacy forced him from his "functional atheism" (as he put it) to seek a God who is known in what he has made.

According to the Bible, every realm of reality — physical, moral, spiritual, cultural — has a certain divinely-ordained structure to them. In some cases, especially in nature, these laws function automatically. The work of gravity, the orbits of planets, and the metamorphosis of a butterfly ... Add your own ideas! We may even say that:

Creation is a sacrament.

God the Trinity is the Creator of the universe and His laws and wisdom oversee it all. We are not surprised, then, if the whole creation — every creature in it, and every particle of it — declare God's glory and make Him known! God has revealed Himself in the person of His son Jesus Christ — His living, incarnate revelation. He has revealed Himself in Scripture — His special, written revelation. He also discloses Himself through creation — His general, natural revelation. Indeed, through faith in Jesus Christ as He is revealed to us in Scripture, we come to understand who God is, and that the world as His creation, speaks of Him everywhere.

Isaiah 6:3 literally reads, "*Holy, Holy, Holy is the Lord of Hosts, the fullness of the earth is His glory.*" Toby Sumpter described it beautifully: "We are inextricably embedded in this world, in the material world. The wind scrapes our faces as much as the branches of low hanging trees. Words and images ricochet through space and time like chisels swung against marble, chipping, shaping, creating, destroying. We are inescapably embodied. We are bodies that act and react as we are acted upon. This means that all of life is already a ritual, already sacramental, already profoundly spiritual. This is because God made the world and upholds it by the Word of his power and by the breath of his Spirit. So where will you go from his presence? Will you hide in a cave, at the bottom of the sea, in outer space?"

Creation has a spiritual intent.

The way we think about creation is foundational to a Biblical view of life. This is not a philosophic or scientific discussion. Sure, it has implications for the creation and evolution debate, but its real significance is spiritual. We can see this in at least a few important ways:

First, it teaches us *who God is.*

It exalts Him as the sovereign, omnipotent, wise, good, and loving Creator.

Second, it teaches us *who we are.*

We learn that the Lord Himself is God; that He made us, and not we ourselves; and that we are His people and the sheep of His pasture (Ps 100:3). The doctrine of creation puts our lives in a proper perspective before God and humbles us.

Third, *it strengthens faith.*

If God can create the world, He can certainly redeem it. If God is the Maker of heaven and earth, He can surely minister to me at my time of need! Creation guarantees new creation both individually and cosmically.

So with John we can only say: "*Worthy art Thou, our Lord and our God, to receive glory and honour and power; for Thou didst create all things, and because of Thy will they existed, and were created*" (Revelation 4:11).

REFLECTIVE QUESTIONS

- Write a paragraph explaining **one** of the passages below.

"For since the creation of the world God's invisible qualities--his eternal power and divine nature--have been clearly seen, being understood from what has been made, so that people are without excuse." (Romans 1:20)

"The heavens declare the glory of God; the skies proclaim the work of his hands. Day after day they pour forth speech; night after night they reveal knowledge." (Psalm 19:1,2)

- What implications does this section have for the way we care for the environment?

4. What is the Image of God ?

"Then God said, 'Let us make man in our image, in our likeness' ... So God created man in his own image, in the image of God he created him; male and female he created them." (Genesis 1:26-27)

What did the writer mean by the idea of being "made in the image of God"? Clearly, he was differentiating between the creation of humanity and all other aspects of creation. In fact, though it might seem a scary way of putting it, he was pointing to an intrinsic "godlikeness" in humanity.

A big claim! But whilst we immediately recognise that we are not gods (!), we often act as if we're the god of our own lives. Again, this idea of image suggests dependency rather than autonomy. The shadow cannot exist without the substance.

It also suggests responsibility. Having been given so much, how then shall we live? To be fully human is to fully reflect God's creative, spiritual, intelligent, communicative, relational, moral and purposeful capacities.

So, what *does* it mean to be created in God's image? The Hebrew root of the Latin phrase for image of God—*imago Dei*—means image, shadow or likeness of God. You are a snapshot of God. At the very least this means humans occupy a higher place in the created order because we alone are imprinted with godlike characteristics. I heard a TV preacher say this, and I don't think he was half wrong, once you think about it: "Your godlikeness is the path to your destiny."

As John Piper put it: **"You are most yourself when the God who made is fully expressed."**

But in what *way* are you an image of God? How are you godlike?

First, the truth about you is that **you are creative because God is creative:** *"In the beginning God created the heavens and the eart*h" (Genesis 1:1).

The second truth about you is that **you are spiritual because God is Spirit**: "*The Spirit of God was hovering over the waters"* (Genesis 1:2). Every human possesses spiritual aptitudes and capacities. We are more than the sum of our physical parts. Our spiritual nature, though unseen, is as real as our physical nature. Nurturing our spirit is as important as eating, drinking and exercising are to our physical body. The very essence of God is spiritual, and that essential quality has been imprinted on humans.

A third truth about you is that **you communicate because God communicates**: "*God said, 'Let there be light'*" (Genesis 1:3). Anthropologists agree that the emergence of symbolic language—first spoken, then written—represents the sharpest break between animals and humans.

A fourth truth about you is that **you are intelligent because God is intelligent**: "*In the beginning was the Word [logos, a Greek word meaning reason, or logic] and the Word was with God, and the Word was God*" (John 1:1).

Logical sequential thought flows from the orderliness of God's mind. As a result, though we are not all intellectuals, we each possess a mind and a way of thinking and learning, so Jesus commanded us to love God with our minds (as well as our hearts and all our strength).

A fifth truth about you is that **you are relational because God is relational:** *"It is not good for man to be alone"* (Genesis 2:18). As we noted before, the phrase, "*Let us* *make man in our image*" reveals an "us-ness" in the very nature of God. The very essence of God is relational, and that essential quality has been imprinted on humans.

A sixth truth about you is that **you are morally responsible because God is a moral being**. *"And the Lord God commanded the man, 'You are free to eat from any tree in the garden; but you must not eat from the tree of the knowledge of good and evil, for when you eat of it you will surely die'*" (Genesis 2:16-17). Just as there are natural laws that govern the universe, universal moral laws govern human behaviour.

When we fully grasp what it means to bear God's image, we are at once struck with both the grandeur and the tragedy of our unrealized possibilities. To be fully human is to fully reflect God's creative, spiritual, intelligent, communicative, relational, moral and purposeful capacities. In God's infinite creativity there are no duplicates; you are the *only* you there has ever been or ever will be.

As a final thought, John Wesley used the idea of "Image of God" thinking to explain the full meaning of salvation and all that it meant.

"By salvation I mean not barely according to the vulgar notion deliverance from hell or going to heaven but a present deliverance from sin a restoration of the soul to its primitive health its original purity a recovery of the divine nature the renewal of our souls after the image of God in righteousness and true holiness in justice mercy and truth."

REFLECTIVE QUESTIONS

- How would you describe the Hebrew idea of the "Image of God" for modern listeners?

- Do you think that Wesley's description of salvation as a "recovery of the divine nature the renewal of our souls after the image of God" is useful? Can you identify with it in your own life?

5. Why does God judge us?

"Remember his marvellous works that he has done; his wonders, and the judgments of his mouth." (Psalm 105:5)

First the good news, then the bad news?

The Bible often links up two ideas that seem, at first, at odds. The first is the creation, the "*marvellous works that he has done*" and the second, less welcome idea is the "*judgements of his mouth.*" I want to think towards the title question through three basic questions that hold those two doctrines (Creation and "Fall") in tandem and enhance our understanding of a Biblical perspective on life.

1. How far did the effects of the Fall spread?

Here's the Wikpedia summary: "In Christian theology, the Fall of Man, or the Fall, is a term used to describe the transition of the first man and woman from a state of innocent obedience to God to a state of guilty disobedience. Although not named in the Bible, the doctrine of the Fall comes from a biblical interpretation of Genesis chapter 3. At first, Adam and Eve lived with God in the Garden of Eden, but the serpent tempted them into eating the fruit from the tree of knowledge of good and evil, which God had forbidden. After doing so, they became ashamed of their nakedness and God expelled them from the Garden to prevent them from eating from the tree of life and becoming immortal."

For many Christian groups (but not all) the doctrine of the Fall is closely related to that of Original Sin. They believe that the Fall brought sin into the world, corrupting the entire natural world, including human nature, causing all humans to be born into original sin, a state from which they cannot attain eternal life without the grace of God. So here's the thing: God created the whole world and all of life, but how much of it has been damaged by our sin?

Some of it, or all of it? Is sin's impact limited or total in scope? The Biblical answer is quite clear: the consequences of sin are comprehensive. Nothing has escaped its crushing effects. Three examples will prove this.

First, the *physical creation* itself has been damaged deeply by sin, as every "natural disaster" suggests.

Second, the *moral and cultural worlds* certainly demonstrate that something somewhere is seriously askew. Family breakdowns are mirrored by political and economic injustice, scientific arrogance and artistic decadence.

Third, our *individual lives* have also been deeply distorted by sin. If the Ten Commandments are taken as a thumbnail sketch of normative moral life, then our regular violations show how deep the distortions go. The Bible's narrative insists that psychological disturbances, physical diseases, and mental illness derive wholly from sin, as initial disobedience morphs and develops into wilful rebellion.

The whole creation and the totality of human life have been corrupted by sin. Some would stress a "total depravity." This means that there is no thing or person that has not been touched comprehensively by the impact of sin. God created all of life and all of life has been polluted by sin.

2. What is the relation between sin and creation?

Has the good creation actually "gone bad" because of sin? Is the world itself now evil after the fall? The Bible's answer is no!

Albert Wolters puts it well: "The central point to make is that, biblically speaking, sin neither abolishes nor becomes identified with creation. Creation and sin remain distinct, however closely they may be intertwined in our experience. ... In short, evil does not have the power of bring to naught God's steadfast faithfulness to the works of his hands."

Evil attaches itself to creation like a cancer and ravages it. Sin deforms the world and makes a caricature of it. Good things are abused by sin, but they are not utterly destroyed. Even in the most perverse situations, the goodness of creation remains intact and always shines through. A bad school is still a school. A broken marriage is still a marriage. A corrupt government is still a government.

The point is that corruption is not creation and we must never confuse the two. There's a difference between a "barn" and the "rats" that infest it! The farmer targets the rats in order to restore his barn to its proper function. In the same way, God aims redemption at sin in order to get his creation back. Sin is an alien invader, contrary to God's purposes. It does not belong. It is incapable of destroying God's handiwork! Creation in any of its forms has not become intrinsically evil. It is in need of redemption.

Bradshaw Frey summed it up well:

"When sin entered the world, its effect was to pervert Creation, not to destroy it. This perversion was thorough and encompassed every aspect of creation, but God did not let the very structure or order of creation tumble. Sin is an alien invasion. It is parasitic. Sin can live off creation, but it cannot replace it."

3. What is "worldliness"?

Christians often define "worldliness" as any realm of life not directly related to the Church. Examples might include such areas as politics, business, art, music, education, journalism, sports, entertainment, work, fashion, food, the media –quite a wide area of activities, really! If an activity is not explicitly spiritual like prayer, Bible study, fellowship, or evangelism, then some would classify it as "unspiritual" and possibly suspect.

However, this is *not* what the Bible means by worldliness. Worldliness consists not in things or realms *per se*, but in their *misdirection* away from God. Fallen human beings regularly abuse what God has made and that is exactly what "worldliness" is: the *perverted* creation.

For example, words are the gifts of God, but they can be easily misused. In complaining about false teaching, St. Augustine said, "I bring no charge against the words which are like exquisite and precious vessels, but the wine of error is poured into them for us by drunken teachers." He carefully distinguishes between the structure of words and their direction. We must do the same. We can bring no charge against anything God has made, but we can distort everything He has made. Worldliness consists in this unfortunate distortion. In short, it is sin.

Now if worldliness consists of making bad use of good things, then godliness consists of making the right use of good things. Believers in Christ have the potential of redirecting every realm of life to its divinely intended purpose, making it holy. We can pour truth into the exquisite vessels of words. We can restore broken relationships. We can challenge political corruption. We can heal broken families. We can renovate corrupt businesses. We can rehabilitate bad schools. The whole of life has the potential of being restored through its proper redirection. Everything God created is good. The fall twisted it all, making it "worldly." Redemption turns all things back toward Him, making them new again! *"Therefore, if anyone is in Christ, the new creation has come: the old has gone, the new is here!"* (2 Corinthians 5:17)

Why does God judge us? The Bible is clear on the point: *"But you are pure and cannot stand the sight of evil.* (Habakkuk 1:13) God judges because he is righteous and holy. In Revelation 4:8, we read about angelic beings coming before the Lord, not resting day or night, and repeating over and over again, *"Holy, holy, holy is the Lord God, the Almighty-the one who always was, who is, and who is still to come."*

The holiness of God forbids the entrance of sin. Many shy away from thinking about God's judgement, though they have no difficulty recognising their own sinfulness or the world's evil. The idea of judgement forces reaction.

4. What are the consequences of a doctrine of judgement?

It warns us. And it is supposed to. When we see what happens to others who disregard what God's Word says, it should cause us to think twice about what we are about to do. As Paul put it in 1 Corinthians10:6: *"Now these things occurred as examples to keep us from setting our hearts on evil things as they did."*

It sobers us. It forces us to reassess the way we have been living our lives and hopefully change our priorities. Though it is a painful awakening, as C. S. Lewis pointed out, "Pain is God's megaphone to rouse a deaf world."

It humbles us. God's judgment strips away our self-righteousness and reminds us about our real state of affairs. It reminds us that we are not really in control of our lives and how we really need God.

It reassures us. The fact that there will be a final judgment reassures us there is justice in the universe. We all know of wicked people in the world who deserve judgment. The wicked will be held accountable for what they have done. And it is reassuring to know there ultimately will be justice.

REFLECTIVE QUESTIONS

- Why are these two doctrines – creation and fall – absolutely essential for understanding the Christian worldview?

- How does the Gospel of Jesus Christ resolve the tension between the doctrines of creation and the fall?

6. What is Covenant?

"I am the Lord your God, who brought you out of the land of Egypt, out of the house of slavery." (Exodus 20:2)

This is how a standard Covenant agreement started out in ancient times, with a statement of who the principal partner was: the one setting out the terms of the agreement.

The Hebrew word for covenant (*berith*) occurs 284 times in the Old Testament and the Greek *diatheke* occurs 37 times in the New Testament. That is to say, it's a crucial concept!

But what does it mean for us? Technically, it just means "Contract," but Henri Nouwen takes it much deeper, in terms of relationship:

"When God makes a covenant with us, God says: 'I will love you with an everlasting love. I will be faithful to you, even when you run away from me, reject me, or betray me.' In our society we don't speak much about covenants; we speak about contracts. When we make a contract with a person, we say: 'I will fulfil my part as long as you fulfil yours. When you don't live up to your promises, I no longer have to live up to mine.' Contracts are often broken because the partners are unwilling or unable to be faithful to their terms.

But God didn't make a contract with us; God made a covenant with us, and God wants our relationships with one another to reflect that covenant. That's why marriage, friendship, life in community are all ways to give visibility to God's faithfulness in our lives together."

Timothy Keller developed Nouwen's discussion in terms of how we understand marriage.

"In sharp contrast with our culture, the Bible teaches that the essence of marriage is a sacrificial commitment to the good of the other. That means that love is more fundamentally action than emotion. But in talking this way, there is a danger of falling into the opposite error that characterized many ancient and traditional societies. It is possible to see marriage as merely a social transaction, a way of doing your duty to family, tribe and society. Traditional societies made the family the ultimate value in life, and so marriage was a mere transaction that helped your family's interest. By contrast, contemporary Western societies make the individual's happiness the ultimate value, and so marriage becomes primarily an experience of romantic fulfilment. But the Bible sees GOD as the supreme good – not the individual or the family – and that gives us a view of marriage that intimately unites feelings AND duty, passion AND promise. That is because at the heart of the Biblical idea of marriage is the covenant."

Marriage works as a metaphor for the real meaning of a Biblical covenant.

How were they set out?

Basically, the pattern is as follows. The initiating party describes himself and what he has done, then there is a list of obligations between the two (or more) parties. What follows is the section dealing with rewards and punishments that govern the keeping and breaking of the covenant.

For example, the Ten Commandments fit this pattern and form a covenant document. First, the initiator states who he is and what he has done: "*I am the Lord your God, who brought you out of the land of Egypt, out of the house of slavery.*" (Exodus 20:2)

Then there is a list of obligations between the two (or more) parties. "*You shall have no other gods before Me,*" (Exodus 20:3). "*You shall not make for yourself an idol . . .* " (Exodus 20:4). "*You shall not take the name of the Lord your God in vain . . .* " (Exodus 20:7).

Then there is the section dealing with rewards and punishments that govern the keeping and breaking of the covenant. " . . . *for the Lord will not leave him unpunished who takes His name in vain,*" (Exodus 20:7).

"Honor your father and your mother, that your days may be prolonged in the land which the Lord your God gives you," (Exodus 20:12).

There are several examples of covenants contained in the Bible but all those between God and man are originated by God and are an act of His grace. Also, Covenants have signs that represent the covenant promises. The Tree of Life (Gen 2:9) was the sign of the Adamic Covenant. The rainbow was the sign of God's covenant with Noah (Gen 9:13). The Mosaic Covenant had the sign of the tablets of the Ten Commandments (Exodus 24:12).

The Bible itself is a covenant document. The Old and New Testaments are really Old and New *Covenants*. The word, "testament," is simply the Latin for Covenant. The New Testament/ Covenant is between Christ and His church. The covenant sign is baptism (Col. 2:11-12) with the continued participation in the covenant via the Lord's Supper (1 Cor 11:25).

The key New Testament chapter for the Christian concept of the New Covenant is Hebrews 8, a portion of which is quoted below:

"For if that first covenant had been faultless, there would have been no occasion to look for a second. For he finds fault with them when he says: "Behold, the days are coming, declares the Lord, when I will establish a new covenant with the house of Israel and with the house of Judah, not like the covenant that I made with their fathers on the day when I took them by the hand to bring them out of the land of Egypt. For they did not continue in my covenant, and so I showed no concern for them, declares the Lord. For this is the covenant that I will make with the house of Israel after those days, declares the Lord: I will put my laws into their minds, and write them on their hearts, and I will be their God, and they shall be my people. And they shall not teach, each one his neighbor and each one his brother, saying, 'Know the Lord,' for they shall all know me, from the least of them to the greatest. For I will be merciful toward their iniquities, and I will remember their sins no more." In speaking of a new covenant, he makes the first one obsolete. And what is becoming obsolete and growing old is ready to vanish away." (Hebrews 8:7–13)

The Christian view of the New Covenant is a new relationship between God and humans mediated by Jesus which necessarily includes all people, both Jews and Gentiles, upon sincere declaration that one believes in Jesus Christ as Lord and God. The New Covenant also breaks the generational curse of the original sin on all children of Adam if they believe in Jesus Christ, after people are judged for their own sins, which is expected to happen with the second arrival of Jesus Christ.

Let's close with a wonderful passage from Paul E. Miller who described what "Covenant Life" might look like for us as believers:

"Everything you do is connected to who you are as a person and, in turn, creates the person you are becoming. Everything you do affects those you love. All of life is covenant.

Embedded in the idea of prayer is a richly textured view of the world where all of life is organized around invisible bonds or covenants that knit us together. Instead of a fixed world, we live in our Father's world, a world built for divine relationships between people where, because of the Good News, tragedies become comedies and hope is born."

REFLECTIVE QUESTIONS

- Mark Driscoll describes the idea of Covenant as "God pursues." Why do you think that is?
- How does the idea of Covenant help us (as modern-day believers) as we consider a) dating b) church life?

7. Why did God become man?

"For we do not have a high priest who is unable to feel sympathy for our weaknesses, but we have one who has been tempted in every way, just as we are – yet he did not sin. Let us then approach God's throne of grace with confidence, so that we may receive mercy and find grace to help us in our time of need.." (Hebrews 4:15-16)

The way we think about Jesus is important.

Is he God or man? ...or both? And in seeking your explanation, with which category do you begin?

In the first couple of centuries of the Church, both approaches were attempted and two kinds of heresies took root: one started off with a straight equation of Jesus=God. He only appeared human but was really divine. His human traits were only apparent. If I can say it respectfully, it was like Superman with the bullets bouncing off him. In this way of thinking, he performed miracles simply because he was God.

This produced the critique of Islam; How could God die?

In the opposite view, Jesus was really man, though filled with the spirit of God and so godly, or divine.

Then subtler explanations were attempted. He was born man but the Spirit came on at baptism and ascended at death (*"Why have you forsaken me?).*

Or how about this one: He had a human body but a divine soul. The trouble is that none of these really satisfy what the Bible itself says

"Being in very nature God..."

"Image of the invisible..."

"He who has seen me has seen the father."

"The Word was God... the Word became flesh..."

It's just not good enough to say that Jesus had a "divine soul" and human body because to be human is not merely bone and tissue. We are what we are inside

And so Jesus (Luke 2:40.51) grew naturally. He was weary, thirsty... he exhibited the normal reactions of a physical body. He *"looked round in anger..."*, he wept, he asked for close friends to stay awake with him. These are the attributes of a sensitive human being.

In Hebrews 2 and 4, the expression of this complete humanity is woven into the total meaning of why God became man. "

"He understands our weaknesses, for he faced all of the same temptations we do, yet he did not sin. So let us come boldly to the throne of our gracious God. There we will receive his mercy and we will find grace to help us when we need it."

He is touched with the feeling of our pain. He can be touched NOW because of what he experienced THEN.

Because, you see, if, so to speak, the bullets bounced off him, then so did the pain. If Jesus has some advantage over me in being human (that it's just an act, a game) then how does he really understand? How did he really "*suffer being tempted*"? You see, he didn't sin. It's hard to understand how he can face the temptation fully if there was no possibility of failure...

But it's at this point that we misunderstand what it is to be human. We think that we are the norm, but really that's not so. For generations the human race has devolved (rather than evolved) into a state of increasing wickedness and darkness. Is it not so?

But we were not created for sin but for God, for pleasure and light. We were created for heaven. Our choices have led us badly astray, worse and worse . Romans 1 describes that spiralling in of sin and degradation.

We have arrived at the point when we almost do not realise that we even face temptation. Or think much of it. And so we blunder from wrong choice to wrong choice.

But Jesus is fresh born from God, the son of God, the second Adam… the *light that lightens everyone* was coming into the world. He was the first truly human being since Adam. He came with two driving passions: one was "*to do the will of He who sent me*" and the other was the overwhelming pain of the people around him. "*He had compassion on them…*" Those two polar drives charged every word and action with powerful meaning.

The divine commission meets the human condition.

So I suggest that Jesus had it not easier but **tougher** than us because he was fully awake to what temptation really was. It was sharper for him. He really "*suffered being tempted*". If you think the pain on the cross was just physical (which I don't), the pain of Gethsemane was deeper than we could ever understand. And he washed the feet of Judas too, that night.

But he is touched with the feeling of our pain because he fully experienced it. "That which is not assumed is not healed" said a wise Athanasius. God entered fully into what it was to be human so that humans might enter fully into what it is to be Godly. And because he understands, he's in a position to help.

But what use is it to be helped by someone who is –after all- in the same position as you? It would be like an AA meeting run by an alcoholic. The leader might mean well, sure, but you just know that it might not work in the long run. You can't trust them, ultimately, to stay clear of the stuff themselves. But Jesus is clear of the stuff. He has faced the temptations but is clear of the sin, of the failure. "*He faced all the temptations we do, yet he did not sin*." That's the difference.

REFLECTIVE QUESTIONS

- Think about the consequences if you over-emphasise a) the God side and b) the human side of Jesus.

- Reflect on this statement: "That which is not assumed is not healed."

8. How does the cross change us?

"Therefore, since we have been justified by faith, we have peace with God through our Lord Jesus Christ.

Through him we have also obtained access by faith into this grace in which we stand, and we rejoice in hope of the glory of God." (Romans 5:1-2)

The centre-point of the Christian faith is the cross of Christ. Why is that? And how does the cross of Christ change the way we live?

John Stott wrote a moving explanation in his book *The Cross of Christ*:

“I could never myself believe in God, if it were not for the cross. The only God I believe in is the One Nietzsche ridiculed as 'God on the cross.' In the real world of pain, how could one worship a God who was immune to it? I have entered many Buddhist temples in different Asian countries and stood respectfully before the statue of the Buddha, his legs crossed, arms folded, eyes closed, the ghost of a smile playing round his mouth, a remote look on his face, detached from the agonies of the world. But each time after a while I have had to turn away. And in imagination I have turned instead to that lonely, twisted, tortured figure on the cross, nails through hands and feet, back lacerated, limbs wrenched, brow bleeding from thorn-pricks, mouth dry and intolerably thirsty, plunged in Godforsaken darkness. That is the God for me! He laid aside his immunity to pain. He entered our world of flesh and blood, tears and death. He suffered for us. Our sufferings become more manageable in the light of his. There is still a question mark against human suffering, but over it we boldly stamp another mark, the cross that symbolizes divine suffering. 'The cross of Christ ... is God’s only self-justification in such a world” as ours....' 'The other gods were strong; but thou wast weak; they rode, but thou didst stumble to a throne; But to our wounds only God’s wounds can speak, And not a god has wounds, but thou alone.”

And how does the Cross "work"? We see how it is the entry of God into the worst of human life, into the most terrible parts of our experience, but how does it effect change in the way we live?

Sacrifice, atonement how does the cross work? How does Jesus dying change me?

Many have offered different theories, and perhaps no single explanation can stand alone.

A Ransom to Satan: This view sees the atonement of Christ as a ransom paid to Satan to purchase man's freedom and release him from being enslaved to Satan.

Recapitulation Theory: This theory states that the atonement of Christ has reversed the course of mankind from disobedience to obedience. It believes that Christ's life recapitulated all the stages of human life and in doing so reversed the course of disobedience initiated by Adam.

Dramatic Theory: This view sees the atonement of Christ as securing the victory in a divine conflict between good and evil and winning man's release from bondage to Satan. The meaning of Christ's death was to ensure God's victory over Satan and to provide a way to redeem the world out of its bondage to evil.

Mystical Theory: The mystical theory sees the atonement of Christ as a triumph over His own sinful nature through the power of the Holy Spirit.

Moral Influence Theory: This is the belief that the atonement of Christ is a demonstration of God's love which causes man's heart to soften and repent.

Example Theory: This view sees the atonement of Christ as simply providing an example of faith and obedience to inspire man to be obedient to God. Those who hold this view believe that man is spiritually alive and that Christ's life and atonement were simply an example of true faith and obedience and should serve as inspiration to men to live a similar life of faith and obedience.

Commercial Theory: The commercial theory views the atonement of Christ as bringing infinite honour to God. This resulted in God giving Christ a reward which He did not need, and Christ passed that reward on to man. Those who hold this view believe that man's spiritual condition is that of dishonoring God and so Christ's death, which brought infinite honor to God, can be applied to sinners for salvation.

Governmental Theory: This view sees the atonement of Christ as demonstrating God's high regard for His law and His attitude toward sin. It is through Christ's death that God has a reason to forgive the sins of those who repent and accept Christ's substitutionary death.

Penal Substitution Theory: This theory sees the atonement of Christ as being a vicarious, substitutionary sacrifice that satisfied the demands of God's justice upon sin. With His sacrifice, Christ paid the penalty of man's sin, bringing forgiveness, imputing righteousness, and reconciling man to God.

All of these theories may possess some aspect of truth. Paul never "spells it out," though in Romans 5 he explores the consequences of the cross: *"We have been justified," "we have peace with God"*, and we *"rejoice in hope of the glory of God."*

It's the past, present and future of our wonderful life with Jesus! When Jesus died on the cross, and when I received that *"by faith"*, then I was "justified". I am now treated "just-as-if-I'd never sinned!"

And so *"We have peace with God."* The war is over, the conditions of surrender have been drawn up. Peace is declared. And that past completed action of the cross brought us into a new place, into the *"grace in which we stand."* And we have gained access only *"by faith."* Nothing to do with how good our performance is, or how clever we are!

And so we rejoice! The Greek word is very strong: it suggests and shouting out in pleasure, whirling about in total abandon. We rejoice not only for this present situation- this grace where we now stand – but we rejoice in the prospect of the glory that is to come! We rejoice *"in hope of the glory of God."*

Peace, grace and glory: what a wonderful supply!

I became a follower of Jesus because of two basic problems. Those problems related to my past, and my future. From the past, I carried the burden of a thousand wrong decisions, with all their sad consequences. From the future I drew all sorts of anxieties and fears.

Guilt for my past and anxiety for my future. That's the alternative to the grace that Jesus offers. What an astonishing life we have been brought into, in Christ. It's a life where I find peace, at last; where I stand in grace and where I anticipate glory now and to come.

REFLECTIVE QUESTIONS

- Go through the various theories offered here and suggest the pluses and minuses of each.

- When you first came to Christ, how did you think about the cross? Has your understanding changed now? If so, in what way?

9. What happened when Jesus rose from the dead?

"But if it is preached that Christ has been raised from the dead, how can some of you say that there is no resurrection of the dead? If there is no resurrection of the dead, then not even Christ has been raised. And if Christ has not been raised, our preaching is useless and so is your faith. More than that, we are then found to be false witnesses about God, for we have testified about God that he raised Christ from the dead. But he did not raise him if in fact the dead are not raised. For if the dead are not raised, then Christ has not been raised either. And if Christ has not been raised, your faith is futile; you are still in your sins. Then those also who have fallen asleep in Christ are lost. If only for this life we have hope in Christ, we are of all people most to be pitied. But Christ has indeed been raised .." (1 Cor 15:12-20)

"So if you're serious about living this new resurrection life with Christ, act like it. Pursue the things over which Christ presides. ... See things from his perspective." (Col 3:1 MSG)

As John Piper put it: "God is most glorified in me when I am most satisfied in Him." I long for five things and they are met in the resurrection of Jesus.

What are the implications of the resurrection of Jesus?

Five "Ifs"

V14: "*If Christ has not been raised, then our preaching is in vain.*" "*. . . and your faith is in vain.*"

V15: If Christ has not been raised, "*we are found to be misrepresenting God because we testified of God that he raised Christ.*"

V17: "*If Christ has not been raised then your faith is futile and you are still in your sins.*"

V18: If Christ has not been raised, then "*those who have fallen asleep in Christ have perished.*"

V19: If Christ has not been raised, then "*we are of all men most to be pitied.*"

Now turn it round.... and the "Ifs" become "Buts"

But Christ IS risen, so we are not in our sins! FORGIVENESS

But Christ IS risen, so our faith is not in vain! FRUITFULNESS

But Christ IS risen, so the apostles spoke Truth! TRUTHFULNESS

But Christ IS risen, so we are not to be pitied but to be envied! SIGNIFICANCE

But Christ is risen, so those who have fallen asleep have not perished but are alive! ETERNAL LIFE

1. I long to be forgiven (V17) Because of the resurrection we are forgiven for our sins. How is the resurrection connected to our forgiveness? Check out Romans 4:25. *"He was delivered over to death for our sins and was raised to life for our justification."* "Everybody needs forgiveness" But Paul says, because Christ rose from the dead, we are no longer in our sins. No longer in them! Imagine that!

2. I long for a fruitful life. Second, from verse 14, instead of saying negatively that our faith is in vain (or fruitless), we can say positively that because of the resurrection our faith is fruitful. Everyone wants to be useful; to feel that they make a difference. It's a feeling that has never changed, in spite of sin. But now that we are no longer in our sins, this longing too is satisfied by the resurrection of Jesus. Paul took it further still: *"The life I live I live by faith in the Son of God who loved me and gave himself for me"* (Galatians 2:20).

3. I long for absolute truth. Third, from verse 15, instead of saying negatively that the apostles are false witnesses about the work of God, we can say positively that because of the resurrection the apostles preach what is true. It's like finding solid ground in the middle of quicksand. I can stand on this truth and even help others too. This is truth itself; it's the truth that I've always longed for. And it sets me free from every kind of doubt and confusion. "*I am the way, the truth, and the life*" (John 14:6).

4. I long for significance. V19: Instead of saying negatively that we are to be pitied, we can say positively that because of the resurrection we are to be envied! Envied! Our preaching is not in vain—it is full, meaningful, valid, valuable, significant. If Christ is not raised, then living for him, doing what he says, following his will is a great delusion. Paul knows this. That's why he ends this whole chapter on the resurrection (v. 58) with the words: "*Be steadfast, immovable, always abounding in the work of the Lord, knowing that in the Lord your labour is not in vain.*"

5. I long for life... and life eternal. Finally, there is the longing that we shall live forever in joy, that we do not come to an empty end after a full and valuable life. v18. So because Christ is raised, those who have fallen asleep in him—those who have died in faith—have not perished. They are alive and will live forever! They live the way Christ lives. They will enter into the joy of their Master. *"So if you're serious about living this new resurrection life with Christ, act like it. Pursue the things over which Christ presides. ... See things from his perspective."* (Col 3:1 MSG)

REFLECTIVE QUESTIONS

Today, let's reflect together on what we enjoy in the resurrection of Jesus.

- Forgiveness
- Fruitful life and ministry
- Authentic truth
- An enviable life
- An Eternal life of joy

10. What is the Church?

"I will build my church." (Matthew 16:18)

If you were to ask people what they think of when they hear the word church you would get many differing responses. Some responses may be accurate and some less so, but most are surprised to learn the Bible's own perspective.

First off, of course, the word "Church" is commonly defined as a building used for public worship.

Alternatively, many would refer to a church as an organization (the Catholic Church, the Church of England, and so forth).

The word church in the Bible comes from the Greek word *ecclesia*, which means an "assembly." Wherever it is used in the Bible it refers to people. It can be a mob (Acts 19:30-41), the children of Israel (Acts 7:38), and the body of Christ (Ephesians 1:22; Ephesians 5:25, 32).

We see the word "church" used three different ways: First, as the body of Christ, the church is often defined as a local group of believers (1 Cor 1:2; 2 Corinthians 1:1; Galatians 1:1-2).

Second, it is defined as the body of believers (1 Corinthians 15:9; Galatians 1:13).

Finally, it is defined as the universal group of all people who have trusted Christ through the ages (Matthew 16:18; Ephesians 5:23-27).

What the church is not:

- **The church is not Jews or Gentiles**

We see three distinct groups of people in the Bible: Jews, Gentiles, and the church (1 Cor 10:31-33; Gal3:26-29). Jews are all born as descendants of Abraham through Isaac (Rom 9:6-7). "Gentiles" refers to non-Jews. When a Jew or a Gentile trusts Christ as their Saviour, they are born again into God's family, become a child of God, and are part of the church. They are no longer a Jew or a Gentile (Galatians 3:26-29). The wall of separation between Jew and Gentile is torn down and they become one body (Ephesians 2:14-16).

- **The church is not the kingdom**

Some mistake the church for a kingdom of Heaven that has already come. But the church inherits the kingdom (Matthew 25:34; 1 Corinthians 6:9; 1 Corinthians 15:47-50). The church is here on earth, but the kingdom of Heaven is not here (Isaiah 9:7; Matthew 5:19-20; Matthew 8:11)

- **The church is not a physical building or business organization**

Too often people describe a church building or organization as the church. This is because they emphasize the facility or organizational hierarchy as what constitutes a church. Most churches are organized in such a way that the public face of a church is seen as a business. It's not.

What is the Biblical view of church?

- **The church is the building or temple of God**

Although the church is not a physical building, believers are referred to as the building or temple of God. Like a physical building, believers also have a Cornerstone; Jesus Christ. The foundation is the prophets and apostles. (Matthew 16:16; 1 Corinthians 3:9-17; 1 Corinthians 6:19; 2 Corinthians 6:6; Ephesians 2:19-22).

- **The church is the bride of Christ**

The Bible makes reference to the church being the bride of Christ (2 Corinthians 11:2; Ephesians 5:25-32). This also alluded to in John 14:1-3 when Jesus talked about making a place at His Father's house for us. This is a direct reference to when a man proposes to a woman and they are engaged. The man goes back to his father's house to build an extension! When it was done, he comes to call for his bride, which symbolizes the resurrection (Matthew 25:1; Revelation 19:7-9).

- **The church has a Spiritual purpose**

The local church or assembly of believers has different roles that God gave to specific believers for the purpose of perfecting or training the believers, doing the work of the ministry, and strengthening of the church body (Ephesians 4:11-14). The roles given in the Bible are apostles, prophets, evangelists, pastors, and teachers. Deacons are also mentioned in Acts 6:1-7 and 1Timothy 3:8-13 as servants to wait upon people with physical needs.

The church body also serves as a local group to resolve conflicts (Matthew 18:15-20) and serve as a court (1 Corinthians 6:1-8). In addition, baptisms and the Lord's Supper or communion are observed by the church body (Acts 2:37-40; 1 Corinthians 11:17-34). Depending on the size of the church body, other ministries are performed by the members of the church as God has gifted each person (Romans 12:3-13; Ephesians 4:1-8).

When Jesus had dinner at Matthew's house He was asked how He could spend time eating with sinners (Matthew 9:9-13). Jesus replied, *"It is not the healthy who need a doctor, but those who are ill. But go and learn what this means: 'I desire mercy, not sacrifice.' For I have not come to call the righteous, but sinners."*

With these words, Jesus described the church. Imperfect people who know they needed a Saviour, working together to build relationships, help those in need, and to glorify God by striving to be like Christ and share his love with others.

If this analysis is reasonable, then how should we think about "church" as we see it today?

Do you not secretly think that ecclesiastical organisation - churches and vicars and things- was a bit of a mistake from the start? In many ways, early Christianity was just the new Judaism, wasn't it? We inherit from Judaism the Law, the synagogue, the Hebrew Bible and all the rest. We call them different things but it's hard to imagine Christianity without its special Sabbath Day, without its special buildings and without its professional priests.

Are these things necessities of the human condition that they always reassert themselves and that therefore God tolerates them?

Come to think of it, Jesus was thrown out of synagogues and was careful not to lay anything down that could be construed as "Law" and was finally got rid of by a zealous and "righteous" bunch of assorted clerics and teachers... So we can hardly make an *a priori*a ssumption that these things must be. Don't you think?

Of course, Jesus accepted the religion of his day, just he accepted everything in the world he lived in, tax, farming, even slavery.... everything except certain attitudes. And if it was the attitudes that raised his ire, is that not because it was there that the things he hated were most evident?

Jesus didn't come to destroy one "jot or tittle" of organised religion. His aims were much more important, and I don't think that those things concerned him very much. When he says "*If you are offering a gift at the altar*" or "*when you fast*" we cannot construe this as orders to take gifts to altars or to fast, any more than his citation of Jonah provides a charter for fundamentalist interpretation! And whatever the "Lord's Supper" really looked like at the time, it surely wasn't what it became. Was it a "religious service" at all? Are you sure?

He left no instructions for liturgy or public prayers. When the disciples, feeling one down in comparison to the super-religious Pharisees ask him to teach them *how* to pray, he says, in effect, "It's as simple as saying 'our Father.'

Now he did say "*I will build my church.*" Fair enough, but don't presume that we know exactly what "church" means. It does not automatically follow that Jesus intended to found anything like the existing denominational structures or even a reunified combination of them. Look at the organisational improvisation that you see going on in Acts and in Paul's letters.... doesn't that prove that Jesus had said nothing that could be used as directions for founding a "church"? The apostles simply adapted Judaism and the things that they were familiar with. Does that mean that the system we see evolving during the New Testament period and subsequently solidified in the first centuries of the church are permanently necessary for Christ's work in the world? Surely not. Isn't all this stuff the wrapping, while the gift lies within?

Some respond to structure with pride....a beautiful sacred place, a polished pulpit performance, the minimum of fuss, heating, seating and eating all happening with breathtaking precision. To others, the very machine-like smoothness of all this is an offence! It discredits the sharpness of Jesus' lordship and his vigorous call to follow and live in discipleship and simple trust.

And the people in the institution waver and feel unsure of themselves. They sing "There must be more than this" and they begin to suspect that if God wanted to do a work in this area, then this building that we may presently glory in just might be the very last place where he'd do it! Doubt sneaks in and the functionaries lose their nerve.

Here's my final question: Is the collapse of an ecclesiastical institution the same as the collapse of Christianity? No Christian would say yes. And yet we seem to anticipate it with pain, anguish and a sense of loss. We gird ourselves to make yet more heroic efforts and painful self-sacrifice to prevent it.

But the only question that we have to answer for our generation is how should we be the people of God today?

REFLECTIVE QUESTIONS

- "Isn't all this stuff the wrapping, while the gift lies within?" Can we distinguish between the two?

- "The question that we have to answer for our generation is how should we be the people of God today?" Here are some words to help us as we formulate an answer to that closing question: Pilgrim, Simple, Mobile, Urgent, *"Blessed broken and given..."*

12. Why do we worship?

"Come, let us bow down in worship, let us kneel before the LORD our Maker." (Psalm 95:6)

"If there is no laughter, Jesus has gone somewhere else. If there is no joy and freedom, it is not a church: it is simply a crowd of melancholy people basking in a religious neurosis. If there is no celebration, there is no real worship."

That's from Steve Brown's excellent study on worship, entitled *Approaching God: Accepting the Invitation to Stand in the Presence of God.*

Worship is as misunderstood a doctrine as any other within the church. Contrary to popular belief, worship doesn't start and finish with "the singing bit" of our church services. The Bible has much to say on this. Even working solely from the verse above we note that worship is (or can be) **corporate** *("Come let us...")*; that it is **reverent** *("...let us bow down")* and that it majors on the **acknowledgement** of who God is *("..the Lord our maker")*. That last point is vital: worship is only determined by God Himself, and not everything we do is acceptable to God as worship just because we are sincere or it makes us feel good.

Hebrews 12:28 tells us that we must "*serve God acceptably with reverence and godly fear*." The Greek word translated "serve" here is a form of the word "worship" and is used 21 times in the New Testament in the context of service and worship.

Another form of the word "worship" is the Greek word *therapeuo*—from which we get the English word "therapy"—and this is most often seen translated "heal" in reference to the healing of others. In the New Testament, this word is seen in every case of Jesus' healings.

Other Greek words translated "worship" are *proskeneuo* meaning "paying homage" (1 Cor14:25), *sebazomai*, meaning "to render religious honour" (Romans 1:25), and *sebomai* meaning "to revere or adore" (Acts 16:14). We see this same word used by Jesus to describe the vain, hypocritical worship of God (Matthew 15:9), reminding us that worship may be phoney.

But true biblical worship is to be first and foremost **reverent** (Hebrews 12:28). This means it is to be done with the understanding of who it is being worshiped. God is holy, just, righteous, perfect, powerful, loving, wrathful etc. Those who wish to worship biblically must worship God as He is revealed in Scripture.

Second, we must worship **in truth** (John 4:24). This means that it needs to line up according to the truths in Scripture. Watch out for additives that may not be God-honouring.

Third, true worship is worship **in Spirit**. Because God is Spirit, true worship is a pure, holy, spiritual worship, the offering of the soul and the homage of the heart rather than merely that of the lips.

Finally, true worship will always produce **a change** in the heart of the worshipper, causing a greater desire to love and obey the God we worship. If worship does not propel us into greater obedience, it isn't worship. F.W Robertson said "There is no love that doesn't shape itself into obedience." True biblical worship of the one true and living God is to be a lifestyle, not a moment in time (1 Corinthians 10:31).

Here's Eugene Peterson's rendition of Romans 12:1-3:

" So here's what I want you to do, God helping you: Take your everyday, ordinary life—your sleeping, eating, going-to-work, and walking-around life—and place it before God as an offering. Embracing what God does for you is the best thing you can do for him. Don't become so well-adjusted to your culture that you fit into it without even thinking. Instead, fix your attention on God. You'll be changed from the inside out. Readily recognize what he wants from you, and quickly respond to it. Unlike the culture around you, always dragging you down to its level of immaturity, God brings the best out of you, develops well-formed maturity in you."

Worship is our whole response to who God is and what God has done. So let's get to the heart of true biblical worship and think through how everything done there is in response to the thing they value most.

In the New Testament, worship means believing the gospel and responding with one's whole life and being to the person and work of God's Son, in the power of the Holy Spirit. Worship' means 'worth-ship': ie. reflecting the worth of the thing or person worshipped. So we could say, if you think that money is the most important thing in your life and has greater worth than anything else for you, that you worship money. In the same way, people can worship Elvis Presley, or Coca-Cola.

So what do you worship? If you value something or someone then what you do is designed around it: eg. to earn more money; or to please the person you value. Thus, another important angle on 'worship' is to see it as 'service': what you do in response to the worth of your thing or person.

These two ideas are inseparable. (In fact, some translations of Psalm 100:2 begin '*Worship the Lord with gladness*', while others begin '*Serve the Lord with gladness*': the Hebrew can be translated either way because both ideas are present in the word).

Why worship God? We worship God for two good reasons: Because of who God is; and because of what God does.

Biblical examples of this kind of worship include Psalm 136 (which looks at several different kinds of God's activity); the various songs of praise in Luke 1; or the scene of heavenly praise in Revelation 4-5. If worship is a response to God, then you can come to him however you feel. Most of the historic liturgies of the church are designed in part to lead you towards God from wherever you are.

So "Take your everyday, ordinary life… and place it before God as an offering."

REFLECTIVE QUESTIONS

- How do you focus on God as you come to a time of worship?
- What is your usual pattern before or at the start of a church service or a time of team worship? Is it a helpful pattern?
- List two or three things which you feel you should work on to help you in the process of worshipping God.
- What did you think worship was before this lesson?
- What have you found challenging or heard for the first time in this lesson?
- What do you want to change about the way you worship God?

13. How do we give?

"Give, and it will be given to you. A good measure, pressed down, shaken together and running over, will be poured into your lap. For with the measure you use, it will be measured to you." (Luke 6:38)

What are the principles of stewardship that are enjoined upon the followers of Jesus? How do we give? It is important to remember that a Christian is under grace and not law. There are no "Shoulds" here, but there are principles that govern action, and the above verse shows this very clearly.

How, for example, does the principle of giving translate into the practice of tithing?

Tithing is mentioned three or four times in the New Testament. Jesus acknowledged that the Pharisees were very careful about tithing (Luke 18:12), and he said that they should not leave it undone (Matthew 23:23; Luke 11:42). Tithing, like other old covenant rules and rituals, was a law at the time Jesus spoke. Jesus criticized the Pharisees not for tithing, but for treating tithing as more important than mercy, love, justice and faithfulness.

The only other New Testament mention of tithing is in Hebrews. The fact that Abraham was blessed by and gave tithes to Melchizedek illustrates the superiority of Melchizedek and Jesus Christ over the Levitical priesthood (Hebrews 7:1-10). The passage then goes on to note that "*when the priesthood is changed, the law must be changed also*" (verse 12).

There was a change of the priesthood from the Levites to Jesus Christ, and this implies a change in the law that assigned the Levites to be priests. How much has been changed? Hebrews says that the old covenant is obsolete. The package of laws that commanded tithes to be given to the Levites is obsolete.

We should honour God by voluntarily returning some of the blessings he gives us — this is still a valid principle, but the only place that a percentage is *required* is within the old covenant.

So what principles govern our actions of giving?

The way we give comes under the grace of God in Jesus. Consequently, we read 2 Cor 9:7: "*Each one must give as he has decided in his heart, not reluctantly or under compulsion, for God loves a cheerful giver.*"

Or consider Acts 20:35: "*In all things I have shown you that by working hard in this way we must help the weak and remember the words of the Lord Jesus, how he himself said, 'It is more blessed to give than to receive.'*"

Again, look at 1 Cor 16:2 "*On the first day of every week, each of you is to put something aside and store it up, as he may prosper, so that there will be no collecting when I come.*"

Acts 2:44-47: "*And all who believed were together and had all things in common. And they were selling their possessions and belongings and distributing the proceeds to all, as any had need. And day by day, attending the temple together and breaking bread in their homes, they received their food with glad and generous hearts, praising God and having favor with all the people.*"

Finally, 2 Cor 8:1-24: "*We want you to know, brothers, about the grace of God that has been given among the churches of Macedonia, for in a severe test of affliction, their abundance of joy and their extreme poverty have overflowed in a wealth of generosity on their part. For they gave according to their means, as I can testify, and beyond their means, of their own accord, begging us earnestly for the favor of taking part in the relief of the saints— and this, not as we expected, but they gave themselves first to the Lord and then by the will of God to us."*

There is no "law" or regulation here, just the reminder of what God is like, of what Jesus said, and the need to care for the vulnerable by intelligent and thoughtful thrift.

The principle is Grace received equals Grace lived.

I want to "reap bountifully". Remember that verse? *"He who sows sparingly shall also reap sparingly; and he who sows bountifully shall also reap bountifully."* 2 Corinthians 9:6.

C.S. Lewis once remarked that "To be a Christian means to forgive the inexcusable because God has forgiven the inexcusable in you."

Grace received should equal grace lived. Jesus denounced the man who was released from a crushing debt, and yet who could not offer the same release to one who owed him a very little. And so the verse leads us into the way that we live. Do we live critically, grudgingly, with eyes squinting in distrust, counting our change and quick to notice every slight or possible offence? Do we stand upon our "rights"?

If so, then we are sowing sparingly, and should expect a poor crop when the tally of our life is drawn up. No. Let's enjoy that word "*bountifully*." It suggests living open-handedly, giving to others the way that God has given towards us.

REFLECTIVE QUESTIONS

- What about other aspects of giving: time, talents and treasure?

- How intentional should you be about your giving? Or should it all be spontaneous?

- Do you feel that you knowingly withhold from the Lord or are you totally "given"?

Bible says 10% or is that just a bench mark.

14. What on earth is the Kingdom?

"He sent them out to proclaim the kingdom of God." (Luke 9:2)

"Thy kingdom come, Thy will be done, on earth, as it is in heaven." (Matt. 6:10)

When Jesus sent his disciples out, it was with the clear mandate to *"proclaim the kingdom of God."* But what did he mean, exactly?

Fifteen hundred years before, God had promised Moses that the Israelites "*will be for me a kingdom of priests and a holy nation*"(Exodus 19:6). In 1 Chr 29:10 and Dan 4:3, the phrase "*Kingdom of the LORD*" refers to the Jewish understanding that God would restore the nation of Israel to their land.

But Jesus was not referring to the nation of Israel but to the rule and authority of God.

The word "kingdom" is a translation of the Greek *basileia* which in turn is a translation of the words *malkuth* (Hebrew). Or "kingship," "kingly rule," "reign", "queen", or "sovereignty" or "God's imperial rule", "God's domain."

The concept of the kingdom of God is the main message of Jesus. The relationship between God and humanity inherently involves the notion of the Kingship of God. The Old Testament forms the backcloth on which the New Testament stage is set, or –to use another picture– it is the root system for the flowering of the church of Jesus.

The view of the kingdom developed during that time included a restoration of Israel to a Kingdom like that od David and the intervention of God in history via a powerful, ruling Son of Man as described by Daniel.

Most Jewish writers imagined a restoration of Israel and either a destruction of the nations or a gathering of the nations to obedience to the One True God.

Up to a point, Jesus stood in this tradition. His association of his own person and ministry with the "*coming of the kingdom*" indicates that he was announcing that God's great intervention in history had arrived, and that he was the agent of that intervention.

But what of his suffering and death? How could God's appointed king be killed? The resurrection established his claim, and the claim of his exaltation to the right hand of God established him as "king."

Jesus' predictions of his return make it clear that God's kingdom is not yet fully realized but in the meantime the good news that forgiveness of sins is available through his name is to be proclaimed to the nations.

Thus the mission of the Church begins, and forms the time-zone between the initial coming of the Kingdom, and its ultimate consummation with the Final Judgment.

Has God's kingly rule and authority already come into the world? Or is it still future? Or is there some sense in which it is both present and future? The teaching of the New Testament is clear: The Kingdom is both "already" but "not yet." It has come, and yet it is coming. It is both present and future.

Several verses in the New Testament teach that God's rule has broken into human history to deliver men and women from the power of sin, death, and Satan. Matthew 12:28-29 is a case in point:

"But if I cast out demons by the Spirit of God, then the kingdom [read: redeeming rule] of God has come upon you. Or how can anyone enter the strong man's house and carry

off his property, unless he first binds the strong man? And then he will plunder his house."

In the context of these verses, Jesus had been accused by the Pharisees of casting out demons by Beelzebub, the prince of the demons. Nonsense, Jesus said. Any kingdom divided against itself cannot stand.

God's Kingdom power and authority was present in Jesus and demonstrated in his every word and in his every deed. Over against falsehood and error, he taught truth, and his powerful teaching was proof positive of the Kingdom's presence.

Over against disease, death and demonic possession, he healed, resurrected, and delivered, and his miracles were also powerful proofs positive of the kingdom's presence. From start to finish, Jesus' entire life and ministry was the expression of God's mighty rule that had broken into history to deliver the creation and its human inhabitants from the curse of sin and death. The rule of God was in Jesus. He was, as ancient church theologians believed, the *Autobasileia*, Himself the Kingdom!

But what does that kingdom look like?

Jesus said, *"My kingdom is not of this world. If it were, my servants would fight to prevent my arrest by the Jewish leaders. But now my kingdom is from another place."* (John 18:36

No, it's a different kind of kingdom, *"from another place."* The kingdom that is "*of this world*" might look like patriotism, or defending a comfortable western society against hordes of invading foreigners. It might look like hatred and fear of outsiders. It might be rich and prosperous, coveting power, political control and human authority. It might look more like a business.

But the kingdom of Jesus is the cross! The cross is the Kingdom – in disguise! Yes, there on the cross, God in Christ conquered sin, defeated death, and triumphed over Satan. Yet it could not have appeared more *unkingly*. Jesus hung there in apparent defeat. There He suffered and died. Satan appears to have won the battle.

Yet by this means, Jesus triumphed over God's enemies and ours, and shares that victory with those who believe. Jesus is *Christus Victor*! By means of this victory, we are restored to God and our true purposes as human beings.

It is the mystery of the Kingdom that makes us new creatures in Christ.

REFLECTIVE QUESTIONS

- Think about the phrase "Already but not yet." What happens if you over-emphasize one or the other?

- How do you respond to this quote? "We need to be politically engaged, but peculiar in how we engage. Jesus and the early Christians had a marvellous political imagination. They turned all the presumptions and ideas of power and blessing upside down." (Shane Claiborne)

- This is how Erwin McManus introduced his church. What do you think? "We're a part of the insurrection, trying to turn Christianity upside down. We're an experimental church: God's research and development arm."

- What do we do about the kingdom on earth?

#0193 - 220816 - C0 - 210/148/5 - PB - DID1556728